The
Eisenhowers

by
Cass R. Sandak

CRESTWOOD HOUSE
New York

Maxwell Macmillan Canada
Toronto

Maxwell Macmillan International
New York   Oxford   Singapore   Sydney

Library of Congress Cataloging-in-Publication Data
Sandak, Cass R.
    The Eisenhowers / by Cass R. Sandak. — 1st ed.
        p.   cm. — (First families)
    Includes bibliographical references and index.
    Summary: Examines the life of the World War II general who became the thirty-fourth president of the United States and describes his relationship with his wife, Mamie.
    ISBN 0-89686-653-X
    1. Eisenhower, Dwight D. (Dwight David), 1890–1969—Juvenile literature. 2. Eisenhower, Dwight D. (Dwight David), 1890–1969—Family—Juvenile literature. 3. Eisenhower, Mamie Doud, 1896–1979—Juvenile literature. 4. Eisenhower family—Juvenile literature. 5. Presidents—United States—Biography—Juvenile literature. 6. Presidents—United States—Wives—Biography—Juvenile literature. 7. Generals—United States—Biography—Juvenile literature. 8. United States—Army—Biography—Juvenile literature. [1. Eisenhower, Dwight D. (Dwight David), 1890–1969. 2. Eisenhower, Mamie Doud, 1896–1979. 3. Presidents. 4. First ladies.]
I. Title.   II. Series: Sandak, Cass R.   First families.
E836.S25   1993
973.921'092—dc20
[B]
                                                                                                93-7807

Photo Credits
All photographs courtesy of UPI/Bettmann, except for page 21, which is from the U.S. Navy.

Macmillan Publishing Company
866 Third Avenue
New York, NY 10022

Maxwell Macmillan Canada, Inc.
1200 Eglinton Avenue East
Suite 200
Don Mills, Ontario M3C 3N1

CRESTWOOD HOUSE

Macmillan Publishing Company is part of the Maxwell Communication Group of Companies.

Produced by Flying Fish Studio

Printed in the United States of America

First edition

10 9 8 7 6 5 4 3 2 1

Contents

The Tide Is Turned

The date was June 6, 1944. The weather had been stormy, and the clouds were low. Visibility on the coast of France was not good. The weather had been so bad, in fact, that the planned invasion of Europe had been postponed for a day. But the outlook for better weather was promising.

The Germans had been expecting some kind of invasion, but they were not sure when it would happen. Nor were they sure where it would happen.

Invasion seemed to be the only way the Allies (United States, Britain, Russia, and other nations) could stop Germany from carrying out its plan to take over the world. The Allied troops had gone ashore in Italy and forced the Italians to surrender. What worked there might well work in France.

The idea for the invasion of German-occupied France was one man's. And that man was Dwight D. Eisenhower. A quiet career soldier, he was a man not well known outside his group of close associates. He had been given a tough assignment. President Franklin D. Roosevelt had appointed General Eisenhower supreme commander of the Allied Expeditionary Forces. In short, Eisenhower was in charge of the war in Europe.

The future of the world would rest on the success or failure of this military operation. Originally named Operation Overlord, the invasion became known as D day by the time it took place.

Fortunately, all of Eisenhower's instincts were good ones. The invasion was almost completely successful. Not many Allied troops were killed, and the Germans were taken by surprise. The Allies were able to capture bridges and railroad lines. Because the Germans could not effectively counterattack, the Allies made great progress.

The D day invasion represented a turning point in World War II. There were still many battles to be fought. But the Allies had made a successful landing. And the German war machine was no longer secure.

It would take another 11 months for the Germans to admit defeat and surrender. But the D day invasion was probably the most significant development of the war. Some historians and military experts regard it as one of the most brilliant strategies of all time.

And it made the name of Dwight David Eisenhower a very famous one throughout the world.

Young Ike

Dwight David Eisenhower was born in a rented house on October 14, 1890, in Denison, Texas. He was the third son of David and Ida Eisenhower. He had two older brothers, Arthur and Edgar. After Dwight came three younger brothers, Roy, Earl, and Milton. Another boy died in infancy. Almost immediately young Dwight was nicknamed Ike. The name stuck with him for his entire life.

Ida Stover and David Eisenhower had met in 1884 while they were students at Lane University. They were married in 1885 at Lane. The college was a religious school run by a Protestant sect known as the River Brethren. Extremely devout people, the River Brethren did not believe in war or military service.

When Ike was only a year old, the family moved to Abilene, Kansas. Eisenhower regarded Abilene as his true hometown. Eisenhower's father worked as an engineer at the local creamery and later as manager of a gas company.

Dwight Eisenhower and three of his brothers. Ike is the one on the right in front.

The Eisenhowers were a poor family, although Dwight did not realize this until he was much older. He just assumed that everyone lived the same way his family did. Their home was a modest frame dwelling with only about 900 square feet of living space to share among the numerous family members. Ike's grandfather, Jacob Eisenhower, lived with the family as well. But the house was spotless.

Ida Eisenhower used part of the dowry money she received from her family to buy a piano. The instrument was one of her most prized possessions, and the family often gathered around the piano to sing hymns. Ike's father held weekly Bible readings in the parlor.

Both Eisenhower parents were deeply religious. David was strict and had difficulty showing affection to his family. Ida was hardworking and thrifty. With help from her sons, she canned the fruits and vegetables they grew. She also taught them to do chores and be useful around the house.

Ike found schoolwork easy, and although no one ever regarded him as an intellectual, he was a decent student. He especially liked spelling and math.

Most of all, Ike liked the outdoors. He enjoyed hunting, fishing, camping, and outdoor cooking. An athletic youth, he played on his school's baseball and football teams. He was also good at acting and appeared in several of the school's amateur dramatic productions.

Ike took part in one of Abilene's most famous fistfights, against an older and larger boy from the wealthier part of town. Ike held out for two hours. Neither boy won. The bout showed early evidence of Ike's determination and guts.

A family portrait taken when Ike (far left) was 10 years old.

In May 1909 Ike graduated from high school. But college cost too much money and the family was poor. So Ike went to work with his father at the creamery. He worked 12-hour days, seven days a week.

Then a friend told Ike about the U.S. Naval Academy at Annapolis, Maryland. It was a famous school and it was free. Ike had thought that a career in one of the armed forces wouldn't be such a bad idea. The academy would give him a good education and prepare him for a job. True, he would have to stay in the military when he graduated. And he would be required to pass tough entrance examinations. He would also have to be recommended for the post by a member of Congress.

Before an injury took him out of the lineup, Ike was a determined football player.

Ike at West Point

Due to circumstances, however, Ike did not go to Annapolis. The academy had an age rule, and at almost 21 Ike would be too old to be admitted. But the U.S. Military Academy at West Point, the army's school, did not have the same restrictions. Eisenhower was therefore able to attend the prestigious military school.

In June 1911, Ike left Abilene to make the three-day train journey to West Point. He was 20. Because he had worked for two years, he was older than most of his classmates. By this time Eisenhower stood almost 6 feet tall. He had blue eyes and blonde hair, although his hair began to thin when Ike was still young. The young man also had a winning smile, a feature that would one day become famous throughout the world.

Everything Ike had heard about West Point turned out to be true. It was a difficult school. The hazing (initiation of new students) was unpleasant, and the teaching methods were strict. In order to learn discipline, for instance, students had to stand at attention for hours. And the studies were not easy.

More than anything, Ike enjoyed the outdoors. He still loved sports, and dreamed of playing on the West Point football team. When he got to West Point, he was too light, but he exercised strenuously to get his weight up and made the varsity team. During his second season on the team, however, Ike suffered a knee injury that ended his football playing forever.

In 1915 Eisenhower graduated from West Point and became part of the full-time army. Never a top-ranking scholar, Ike just missed being in the upper one-third of his graduating class. Of the 265 students who entered the class of 1915, only 164 graduated. It was, however, a distinguished class. Of Ike's classmates, 59 eventually rose to the rank of general. And Eisenhower and Omar Bradley became five-star generals.

Mary Geneva Doud

Eisenhower was assigned to Fort Sam Houston, near San Antonio, Texas. No sooner had he arrived there than he met a young woman who had just completed finishing school. Mary Geneva Doud was from a prominent and wealthy family from Denver, Colorado, who spent their winters in San Antonio. She was the second of four daughters born to Min and John Doud and she was known to one and all as Mamie. Mamie was a pretty and lively 18-year-old.

Mamie had been born in Boone, Iowa, in 1896. Her parents then moved to Denver. Mamie's father owned a successful meat-packing business.

Mamie Doud in 1915, the year Ike met her

Ike and Mamie's wedding portrait, 1916

Ike and Mamie were engaged on Valentine's Day in 1916 and married the following July 1 at the Doud family home in Denver. Ike wore his white West Point uniform and cut the cake with his sword.

The Eisenhowers set up housekeeping in San Antonio. Ike believed that an army man's first priority was to serve his country. His family had to come second. He also believed that an army wife's main job was to serve her husband well.

Mamie accepted her husband's demands graciously, putting Ike's position and career above everything else. She was popular both with Ike's colleagues and with their wives. In a short time their apartment became known as Club Eisenhower.

13

Eisenhower was next assigned to Georgia to train soldiers. Almost as soon as the Eisenhowers got there, the United States entered World War I, in April 1917.

On September 24, Mamie Eisenhower gave birth to a son, Doud Dwight Eisenhower. Almost immediately he was nicknamed Icky. The Eisenhowers' happiness was short-lived, however, as the boy became sick at Christmas 1920 and died of scarlet fever in January 1921. Icky was just over three years old. Both Eisenhowers were heartsick, and this loss affected their lives for many years.

In October 1918 Eisenhower was made a lieutenant colonel. He wanted very much to get an assignment overseas and fight on behalf of the United States. But before he could go, the war ended. The armistice was signed on November 11, 1918.

The Peacetime Army

Now Eisenhower was faced with a career decision. With the war over, the peacetime army would be reduced in size. The army had been good to him, and he enjoyed his life as a soldier. But would there be enough of a challenge for him? Could he make a lifetime career of military service? He made a positive decision. And for more than 20 years, Ike served his country in the peacetime army.

Ike and Mamie were sent to Panama from 1922 to 1924. The pain over the loss of their first son was soothed when Mamie gave birth to another boy, John, on August 3, 1922.

Between 1924 and 1929 Eisenhower was dispatched to a variety of assignments both in the United States and over-

The Eisenhowers shortly after their marriage

seas. The family lived in Colorado, Kansas, and Georgia. In 1928 Eisenhower was given a choice between a posting in the United States and one in Europe. He chose the United States, but Mamie intervened. For once she got her way, and the couple went to Paris for several months.

In 1929 Eisenhower got his first close-up look at government. The family moved to Washington, D.C., where Eisenhower worked in the office of the assistant secretary of war.

Son John joins Ike and Mamie in the Philippines.

For about 15 years Eisenhower was content with his career and position as a major. He was hardly a world figure, but he was basically a happy person.

Then in 1935 General Douglas MacArthur ordered Eisenhower to the Philippines. Ike was reluctant to go but eventually did. Mamie refused to join Ike until 1936, when she and 14-year-old John sailed out. They remained there until the end of 1939. Around the time the Eisenhowers celebrated their 25th wedding anniversary, their son received an appointment to West Point. Both parents could not have been more proud.

In the meantime, events were happening in Europe that would change the world forever.

A New War
on Two Fronts

In September 1939 Adolf Hitler's forces marched into Poland. Shortly after that they occupied France and other parts of Western Europe. Not only was war raging in Europe, but on the other side of the world the Japanese began their aggressive stance.

In December 1941 the Japanese staged a surprise attack on the American naval forces based at Pearl Harbor in Hawaii. In a stirring address to Congress and the nation, President Franklin D. Roosevelt issued a declaration of war. Because of Eisenhower's past experience in the Philippines, General George Marshall asked him to advise the army how to help with the military situation there.

In fact, the U.S. forces were badly defeated by the Japanese in the Philippines. General MacArthur blamed Eisenhower for the loss, but defeat there would probably have happened anyway. And Marshall was pleased with Eisenhower's performance in the Pacific. He thought that Ike's military expertise was needed in Europe.

By 1942 Eisenhower had been made a major general. In June of that year he was appointed commander of the European Theater of Operations. He left for Europe and was based in London. One of his first tasks was public relations: He needed to improve the British perception of American soldiers stationed in England.

An Englishwoman named Kay Summersby was assigned to be Eisenhower's driver. An intense friendship grew up between Eisenhower and Summersby. It seems that the two may have had a more serious relationship, but only Summersby's memoirs mention it. On this point, Eisenhower refused to speak.

Eisenhower was to be apart from his wife for nearly four years. While her husband was in Europe, Mamie lived in an apartment in Washington, D.C. John spent his summers and holidays with her there. Ike thought his hotel in London was too expensive and not to his liking, so he moved to a small country house.

Eisenhower was virtually unknown when he went to England. He was 52 years old. As commander of the European Theater of Operations, he was in charge of coordinating the war effort of all the Allied forces in Europe. Virtually the entire Continent—including some of the most highly developed nations in the world—had fallen prey to the advances of Hitler's army.

Only Great Britain and the Soviet Union remained unconquered. Their freedom had cost them many heavy losses. A few other countries maintained neutrality, but that status would be short-lived if the Germans could not be stopped.

There were significant pockets of resistance forces—workers who secretly fought against the Germans, often under dangerous conditions. In France, in particular, there was a strong resistance movement. In addition, the Free French forces under Charles de Gaulle were operating from London.

Eisenhower knew instinctively that the only way to conquer the Germans was to prepare a land invasion of

Ike visits troops at the front in 1944.

France. Troops would then advance across the occupied country toward Germany and finally defeat Hitler's army. From the moment that Ike was appointed commander, every effort was made to achieve that goal. Many of the American troops were inexperienced, so Eisenhower needed to build up his forces to do the job.

But first the Allied forces resolved to weaken the Germans in North Africa. Although Ike seriously doubted the wisdom of this plan, he was put in charge of the invasion of northern Africa. Ike led the troops in the attack. In fact, the North African campaign was a major and costly disappointment, and Ike's original feelings proved right.

During the North African campaign, President Franklin D. Roosevelt visited the front. While meeting with Eisenhower there, Roosevelt informed him that he would be put in charge of planning the Allied invasion of Europe, by now code-named Operation Overlord.

In 1945 Eisenhower delivered the most famous speech of his career. He addressed Londoners and underscored the common bonds of commitment to freedom, liberty, and equality shared by Britain and the United States. Journalists gushed that the speech was another Gettysburg Address. They likened the war hero to Abraham Lincoln, another figure from America's heartland. "He has the Lincoln touch," one writer stated. None of this would hurt Eisenhower's political prospects in the years ahead.

Eisenhower's son, John, graduated from West Point during the last days of the war. Shortly after D day, John came to Europe to visit his father. Like his father in World War I, John desperately wanted to participate in the fight-

General Eisenhower outlines military strategy to American troops just before the D day landing.

ing. The senior Eisenhower would have had to give his permission for John to see active duty. But Eisenhower refused to give preference to his son, so John did not fight in World War II. Ike was secretly relieved.

D day was a major success. It took almost a year for the Allied forces to reach the German borders. But by the spring of 1945, Germany's cities—including the once-proud capital, Berlin—were in ruins. Hitler's headquarters had been destroyed, and Hitler himself committed suicide.

On May 7, 1945, the Germans surrendered. Eisenhower's decisions in the last year of the war had been remarkably perceptive. As a result of his skill and courage, he became a world hero.

Ike in Peacetime

Eisenhower returned to the United States in June 1945. More than two million cheering Americans gave the hero a ticker-tape parade down New York City's Wall Street. Eisenhower's wife hadn't seen him for almost four years. He wanted only to be reunited with Mamie and to pursue pastimes such as painting and fishing. But Ike was now so popular and busy that he had little time for Mamie.

During this period rumors arose that Mamie had a drinking problem. No one has ever substantiated the stories. It appears that Mamie suffered from Ménière's disease, an inner ear disturbance. This condition caused her to lose her balance and made her seem unsteady on her feet.

Although the war was over, Eisenhower was needed again in Europe, to help clean up the devastation. John joined him, but Mamie remained at home. By now Ike had risen to the highest possible rank: five-star general. After returning to the United States in November 1945, Eisenhower became chief of staff of the U.S. Army.

In June 1947, Mamie and Ike were overjoyed when their son married Barbara Thompson. The daughter of an army man, she would have a good idea of what being an army wife meant. The following year John and Barbara presented the older Eisenhowers with their first grand-child, Dwight David II (known as David). Three daughters came later: Barbara Anne in 1949, Susan Elaine in 1951, and Mary Jean in 1955.

On February 7, 1948, Eisenhower retired from the U.S. Army. In the same year he became president of New York's

Eisenhower while he was president of Columbia University

prestigious Columbia University. Although Eisenhower was not an intellectual, he was a good organizer. His years in the army had taught him patience and tolerance when there were difficult jobs to be done. In addition, Eisenhower's interest in world peace and foreign relations stood him in good stead during his Columbia tenure. But many people regarded Eisenhower as a poor college president. Some of his academic colleagues even saw him as undereducated and overopinionated.

During this period just after the war, influential people began to talk about Ike as a possible presidential candidate. Many of them even began to talk *to* Ike about becoming president. Eisenhower kept turning them down, however, since he was never a very ambitious man. But his popularity just seemed to increase.

Also in 1948 Eisenhower's war memoirs were published. Called *Crusade in Europe*, the book was a best-seller. After the war, too, Eisenhower had time to pursue one of his favorite pastimes: painting.

In 1950 the world shuddered at the prospect of war once more. In Korea the Communist soldiers from the north crossed the 38th parallel. The movement of troops infringed upon southern (non-Communist) territory, and the two groups began fighting. The tensions in Korea were felt in Europe, too. The Eastern European countries had come under Communist control after World War II, and the nations of Western Europe feared a Soviet attack. One result was the formation of the North Atlantic Treaty Organization (NATO). The 12 members agreed to band together for mutual defense—an attack on one would be considered an attack on all. Who better to lead the organization than Eisenhower? And so in early 1951 Ike went once more to Europe, this time as commander of the NATO forces.

During the NATO meetings the Eisenhowers lived in Paris in an elegant palace. There they entertained and were entertained by European royalty and heads of state. In their garden Mamie raised corn for Ike. It was one of his favorite foods, but it wasn't grown in France.

Ike the Politician

In 1952, a presidential election year, the country was looking for a new leader. Truman declined to seek reelection, and the Democrats were not united behind any candidate. Eisenhower did not seem to have many qualifications, though. After all, his experience had been in the military, not in government. Of course, that is exactly what George Washington's background had been. And a number of other presidents before Eisenhower had been soldiers as well. The last president who had served as an army general was Ulysses S. Grant. Grant's military career, in fact, was basically his only qualification for being elected president, in 1868.

It was while the Eisenhowers were in Paris for the NATO meetings that a delegation of Republican party officials urged Ike to seek the Republican nomination for president.

Accordingly, Eisenhower resigned from NATO and began to plan his 1952 campaign carefully. In June he gave his first political speech, in his hometown of Abilene, Kansas. By July he had had a tremendous impact on the nation. At the Republican convention in Chicago, he won the nomination. He named Richard M. Nixon as his vice presidential running mate.

With Mamie at his side, Ike campaigned strenuously. Their campaign train was named *Look Ahead, Neighbor*. The Eisenhowers traveled 50,000 miles through 45 states, and Ike spoke in some 230 towns.

The Eisenhowers just after Ike learned he had won the Republican party presidential nomination in 1952

Suddenly Mamie became as well-known as her husband. Millions of American women copied Mamie's hairstyle and sported Mamie bangs. A shy and retiring person, Mamie Eisenhower had to appear in public and even speak in front of large audiences. The role did not come easily to her, but because she was an army wife she had learned how to handle almost any awkward situation.

During the campaign Nixon was charged with mishandling funds given to his campaign, using the money for personal expenses, and accepting expensive gifts. With Eisenhower's prodding, Nixon went on television to defend himself. Claiming that he had only accepted a cocker spaniel named Checkers for his two girls and that his wife proudly wore a modest cloth coat, Nixon appealed to the public for support. The address became known as Nixon's Checkers speech, but the negative publicity tended to distance Eisenhower from his running mate.

All over the country "I Like Ike" became a rallying cry. It was a catchy campaign slogan that would help catapult the war hero into the White House. Eisenhower was running against Adlai Stevenson, a Democrat. A spirited intellectual who had been divorced, Stevenson did not command the folksy touch of the war hero and his popular wife. On election day the Democrats were left far behind. Eisenhower garnered 34 million popular votes, while Stevenson won only 27 million.

The Eisenhowers leave the Capitol on the president's inauguration day in 1953.

President Eisenhower

On January 20, 1953, Dwight David Eisenhower was sworn in as the nation's 34th president. He was 62 years old. Mamie was sure that the stress of the job would kill him.

Not surprisingly, Eisenhower's inauguration speech centered on the dangers of war and the need to keep world peace. He also denounced the evils of communism. Ike raised his arms high and gave his traditional V for victory sign. The crowd went wild.

The Eisenhower years were a period of unprecedented peace and prosperity for the American people. But the 1950s were also a time of severe tension between the two superpowers, the United States and the Soviet Union.

The Soviet Union had won many of the final victories in World War II. With these victories came Soviet dominance throughout much of the world. And with them came the fear that communism would take over the Western democracies. This period was known as the cold war.

In early 1953 the Soviet leader, Joseph Stalin, died. It was hoped that changes in the Soviet Union would help to reduce tensions between the superpowers.

During most of Eisenhower's years in office, Americans continued to be scared of the Soviets. Anticommunist feeling was on the rise. Largely as a result of a perceived threat of Soviet supremacy, Communists in the United States were hunted out and punished.

Joseph McCarthy, Republican senator from Wisconsin, led a one-man crusade against Americans who may have been Communists, particularly those in the public eye.

Often unfairly, he challenged people who had liberal political views or who would not criticize communism. He also
challenged the patriotism of General George Marshall,
secretary of state under President Truman. Privately
Eisenhower was sickened by McCarthy's tactics. But
publicly he said nothing.

One of Eisenhower's first duties as president was to
bring an end to U.S. involvement in the Korean War. During
the campaign he had promised the voters that he would go
to Korea in search of peace. And he did just that. The peace
was not an easy one, but on July 17, 1953, a truce was signed
that ended the war.

The need to control the spread of atomic weapons
quickly became another issue in the Eisenhower years.
His brainchild was called Atoms for Peace. Under this plan,
the United States would lend uranium, which is used in
making nuclear bombs, to other countries—but they would
be allowed to use the substance only for peaceful purposes.

Eisenhower was a man of peace who favored military
strength only as a way to maintain peace. His warnings
against overspending for defense may have been unex-
pected from an ex-military man. Excessive expenditures on
weapons would only undermine our way of life, he felt.

Mamie's fear that the job of president would hurt Ike
seemed to come true. Eisenhower was in his mid-60s, and
ill health began to bother him. In September 1955 he suffered a major heart attack. He and Mamie were vacationing
at Mamie's family house in Colorado. Mamie called a
doctor. Ike was rushed to an army hospital in Denver. He
spent seven weeks there. During that time, Mamie lived in

30

a nearby room in the hospital. Through care and rest, though, Ike was able to recover. By February 1956 doctors had predicted a full recovery for Eisenhower. Ike was 65.

A Second Term

By the summer of 1956, Eisenhower was well enough to campaign for reelection. His opponent was again Adlai Stevenson, and this time Ike won by 35 million votes to Stevenson's 26 million. Eisenhower's second inauguration actually took place in the White House. Because of bad

"I Like Ike" was the favorite slogan in both of Eisenhower's presidential campaigns.

weather, the official swearing-in was held in the East Room. It was a small ceremony that was later reenacted on the Capitol steps.

During Ike's second campaign an international incident had arisen when the Egyptians tried to take control of the Suez Canal away from the British and the French. Both countries had long-term interests in the canal and in Egypt, but Egyptian nationalism was strongly against the European powers. Eisenhower wanted to keep the United States out of the dispute. Eventually the United Nations intervened and resolved the conflict.

In 1957 the Soviets launched *Sputnik I* into space. It was the earth's first artificial satellite. Americans had not realized how advanced the Soviets were in science and technology. As a result, a new fear gripped the nation: The United States was lagging behind its chief rival for world power.

In the same year civil rights activism began to be a major issue. In his first term Ike had completed the racial integration of the armed forces. But school desegregation, especially in the Deep South, presented a much more difficult problem. Eisenhower shied away from the issue, although he did send federal troops to Little Rock, Arkansas, to enforce a court desegregation order. Generally, however, Eisenhower claimed that civil rights should be handled by the individual states and not by the federal government. It is one of the few blots on Eisenhower's record that he refused to take a more active role in fighting for integration.

In 1957 Eisenhower was sick once more. This time he suffered a stroke. But it was not a serious one, and Eisenhower was able to resume his duties quickly. He knew that he would be retiring in just a few years, and he looked forward to having time to fish, paint, and play golf.

Late in Eisenhower's second term, an incident occurred that threatened to destroy all his hard work to keep Soviet–U.S. relations strong. An American U-2 fighter plane was shot down over Soviet territory. The pilot, Francis Gary Powers, was captured. Although U.S. officials at first denied that the plane was on a spy mission, they were later forced to admit the truth. The episode was another unfortunate legacy for Eisenhower's presidency.

One of Eisenhower's proudest achievements was a strong economy. The economy, which had been geared up for war, was shifted to peacetime activities. But it had not lost its momentum. A large majority of the American people could afford new homes, new cars, and other consumer goods. Jobs were plentiful. Not since the 1920s had the country experienced such a boom, and this time the prosperity was far more widespread.

The Eisenhower White House

In their nearly 36 years of marriage before Ike became president, he and Mamie moved around constantly. As a result of Ike's various military assignments, they had lived in some 27 homes. For the Eisenhowers the White House became the most stable home of all. They lived there longer than anywhere else up to that time.

Used to army discipline, Eisenhower was up regularly at 6:00 A.M. He dressed and read the papers while he ate a light breakfast. Usually he went to his office at 8:00 A.M. Many days he ate his lunch while working. In the afternoon—provided there was no work to be done—Eisenhower often played golf.

Mamie Eisenhower was a woman of simple needs. Her principal pleasures were playing cards and spending time with her family. Much of the excitement at the Eisenhower White House came from John and Barbara's four children. The youngest of these, Mary Jean, was actually baptized in a White House christening.

Deeply in love, Mamie once said of her husband that he was "the spiffiest man" she'd ever seen. Mamie never became interested in politics and saw her role as first lady solely as the president's hostess. For her, being first lady was just like being an army wife.

During their years in the White House, in fact, Ike and Mamie seemed closer—and more in love with each other—than ever. The Eisenhowers had a custom-made double bed

The Eisenhowers share Thanksgiving turkey with their granddaughter Susan.

*In the 1950s television began to play an important part in American lives—
even the first family's.*

in their joint bedroom. It was refreshing to have Mamie tell the world that if she got lonely, she could just "reach out and touch that bald head." The Eisenhowers were incredibly popular with their fellow Americans. Part of their strength was that they seemed, in some ways, just like so many other Americans. Although as first family the Eisenhowers entertained often, they were more content to watch television in the evening. A film—shown in the White House—was their weekly treat.

The first family lived in the executive mansion's private quarters. But certain historical rooms were shown to the public for the first time. Mrs. Eisenhower set aside the Gold Room to house the White House silver and gold plate collection. She was also the first to set aside parts of the White House as "museum" areas.

Mamie Eisenhower presided over the mansion's 132 rooms with skill, ease, and grace. During their eight years in the White House, the Eisenhowers entertained 26 kings, as well as numerous other leaders. In 1957 the queen of England, Elizabeth II, and her husband, Prince Philip, paid a state visit to the Eisenhowers. They stayed at the White House in the same rooms that the queen's parents had occupied when they visited in 1939. Most visitors would have stayed in nearby Blair House, but an exception was made for the royal couple. Eisenhower was quoted as saying that the visit was one he truly hated to see end.

Mamie's White House decor was largely pink and floral. Pink was Mamie's favorite color and was seen often in the clothes she wore as well as in the decoration of the house. Most people who visited the family quarters thought Mamie had lightened the mood successfully. A color was even known as "Mamie pink" for a time during the Eisenhowers' greatest popularity.

In 1959 Mrs. Eisenhower led a distinguished tour through the White House. Eight of her guests were sons and daughters of former presidents of the United States. Beginning with descendants of Grover Cleveland, the guests were able to revisit rooms they had known as younger people.

Christmas was a particularly important time for the Eisenhowers. Mamie's decorations at the White House were known and admired the world over. At Christmas 1958 there were reported to be 27 decorated trees in the executive mansion. Mamie also had a loudspeaker system play Christmas carols so that passersby could hear them. Because of their four grandchildren, Christmas at the White House was a lively time for the Eisenhowers.

During the Eisenhower administration the well-known Easter egg rolling contest on the White House lawn was resumed. The tradition had begun with Rutherford Hayes but had been abandoned during World War II.

By the Eisenhowers' time at the White House, the household staff had grown to almost 500 people. But each year the Eisenhowers gave a single party for all these people. And everyone loved it.

In his spare time Eisenhower relaxed with his golf clubs. He found a space on the White House lawn for a putting green. His other pastime was painting. For Christmas he often gave prints of his paintings as presents.

38   *Mamie waves goodbye from the White House as her husband leaves to attend a ceremony honoring his 70th birthday.*

The Eisenhower years at the White House were marked by several "firsts." Eisenhower's press conferences were the first to be televised. In 1960 Eisenhower became the oldest president, when he celebrated his 70th birthday at the White House.

And Eisenhower was the first executive to use helicopters for transportation. Choppers took the Eisenhowers back and forth to their weekend retreat at Camp David in Maryland. Named for Eisenhower's grandson, the camp is about 90 miles from the White House. The retreat had been a favorite spot of Franklin D. Roosevelt, when it was known as Shangri-La.

After the White House

Eisenhower had hoped to leave a Republican in office when he retired in 1961. The logical successor was Richard M. Nixon, Ike's vice president. But in the close election of 1960, Nixon was defeated. John F. Kennedy, representing a new generation of Democrats, went to the White House.

Eisenhower was never overly fond of Nixon. Among other things, Eisenhower may have remembered the "Checkers" incident of the 1952 campaign. Eisenhower's lack of enthusiasm for Nixon may have cost the Republicans the 1960 election. And when Eisenhower finally did back Nixon, it was too little, too late.

When Eisenhower stepped aside to let Kennedy take over the presidency, he could confidently say, "America is today the strongest, the most influential, and most productive nation in the world."

Mamie and Ike quietly retired to their farm in Gettysburg, Pennsylvania. Apart from the White House, the farm was the Eisenhowers' first real home. Mamie once described it as "no decorator's dream."

At the Gettysburg farm Ike was able to supervise the raising of cattle and crops. The Eisenhowers had originally bought the farm in 1950. Gradually they added land to it until there were more than 500 acres. Old friends and dignitaries came to visit the Eisenhowers there. As always, Mamie entertained graciously and comfortably.

The Eisenhowers enjoyed peace and quiet together at last. But Ike's last years were plagued by a series of small heart attacks. In April 1968 Eisenhower suffered yet another seizure. Gradually his condition worsened, and he was moved to Walter Reed Hospital in Bethesda, Maryland. There he remained for the rest of his life, unable to function well enough to be brought home to his farm.

At his second inauguration, in 1957, Ike had introduced his grandson, David, to Julie Nixon, Richard Nixon's younger daughter. Romance blossomed, and in 1968 the couple married. Eisenhower was too weak to attend the ceremony, but he watched it on closed-circuit television. Two famous political families were now linked.

The end came peacefully for Ike on March 28, 1969.

After his death, Eisenhower's coffin lay in state in the Bethlehem Chapel in Washington's National Cathedral. His remains were then carried by military caisson to the Capitol Rotunda, where his body—in full military dress—lay in state another 24 hours.

Family, friends, and heads of state pay tribute as Eisenhower's casket is carried into Washington's National Cathedral.

Dignitaries from around the world came to pay their respects. Representatives from 78 countries arrived. One of Eisenhower's great colleagues from his World War II days, France's Charles de Gaulle, was in attendance.

From the Capitol, the procession returned to National Cathedral for a solemn funeral. A train then carried Ike's body to Abilene, Kansas, where he was buried on April 2.

Mamie lived on at the Gettysburg farm after Ike died. Barbara and John Eisenhower and their children had a home only about a mile away. When asked how she wanted to be remembered, Mrs. Eisenhower replied that she hoped people would think of her "as a friend." It was a warm and revealing response from a former first lady whom many had come to perceive as distant and reclusive. But it seems as if her shyness was mistaken for aloofness.

Mrs. Eisenhower outlived her husband by ten years. She kept almost completely out of the public eye. Her health was never robust, and she spent long periods every day resting. Mamie suffered a stroke in September 1979 and died in November. Her remains were taken to Abilene, where they lie next to those of her beloved husband.

At the Eisenhower Center in Abilene, there is a museum and library devoted to Dwight D. Eisenhower. Displayed there are many of the documents relating to his military and political career. The family home there was restored as early as 1947. By then Ike had become a famous native son. And he had not yet served as president.

The
Eisenhower Legacy

Eisenhower's personality was relaxed, steady, and confident. He was always popular among his peers because he never had any ambition to be better than others and had no anxiety about success.

Eisenhower was one of the few presidents who had had no political experience before taking office. Most of the nation's presidents had had decades of service in the government by the time they were elected. Eisenhower's training and career were those of a professional soldier. He had never held an elected office or taken part in politics.

Eisenhower represented a combination of geniality and toughness. A brilliant military strategist, he became one of the most decorated soldiers in history. Yet he was almost totally without the arrogance and pride that so often mark military personalities. He tried to minimize human losses while achieving victory over the enemy.

When the Eisenhowers came to the White House, Americans were delighted. The Eisenhowers were not sophisticated, but they seemed to stand for the simplicity and dignity that Americans were longing for. It is difficult, 40 years later, to remember how much the public really liked this first family. Their popularity went hand in hand with prosperous times for most of the nation.

Eisenhower was a military man who was not afraid to put down his sword. There was no question of his tough-

Eisenhower in 1955 at Gettysburg. He was there to honor the memory of Americans who gave their lives in all wars.

ness. But he easily made the shift to civilian service with grace and skill, first as president of Columbia University, then head of NATO, and finally as president of the United States. He was a man who stood for honor and decency.

For Further Reading

Anthony, Carl Sferrazza. *First Ladies: The Saga of the Presidents' Wives and Their Power, 1789-1961.* New York: William Morrow and Company, 1990.

Cannon, Marion G. *Dwight D. Eisenhower: War Hero and President.* New York: Franklin Watts, 1990.

Darby, Jean. *Dwight D. Eisenhower: A Man Called Ike.* Minneapolis: Lerner Publications, 1987.

Ellia, Rafaela. *Dwight D. Eisenhower: 34th President of the United States.* Ada, Oklahoma: Garrett Educational Corporation, 1989.

Fisher, Leonard Everett. *The White House.* New York: Holiday House, 1989.

Friedel, Frank. *The Presidents of the United States of America.* Revised edition. Washington, D.C.: The White House Historical Association, 1989.

Hargrove, Jim. *Dwight D. Eisenhower.* Chicago: Childrens Press, 1987.

Klapthor, Margaret Brown. *The First Ladies.* Revised edition. Washington, D.C.: The White House Historical Association, 1989.

Lindsay, Rae. *The Presidents' First Ladies.* New York: Franklin Watts, 1989.

The Living White House. Revised edition. Washington, D.C.: The White House Historical Association, 1987.

Menendez, Albert J. *Christmas in the White House.* Philadelphia: The Westminster Press, 1983.

St. George, Judith. *The White House: Cornerstone of a Nation.* New York: G. P. Putnam's Sons, 1990.

Sandberg, Peter Lars. *Dwight D. Eisenhower.* New York: Chelsea House, 1986.

Index